JOKES
FOR
KIDS

ARCTURUS

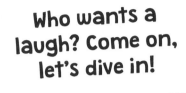

Who wants a
laugh? Come on,
let's dive in!

This edition published in 2019 by Arcturus Publishing Limited
26/27 Bickels Yard, 151–153 Bermondsey Street,
London SE1 3HA

Author: Joe King
Jacket illustrator: Lyudmyla Kharlamova at Shutterstock
Interiors illustrator: Genie Espinosa
Editor: Kait Eaton at Duck Egg Blue
Designer: Duck Egg Blue

ISBN: 978-1-78950-404-0
CH007211NT
Supplier 29, Date 0719, Print run 8467

Printed in China

CONTENTS

JOLLY JUNGLE

What is large and has three trunks?

An elephant going abroad!

What do you call a show full of lions?

The mane event.

Why do monkeys love bananas so much?

They're so a-peeling!

Why should you never trust a giraffe?

They are always telling tall stories.

What ice-cream does a gorilla like best?

Chocolate chimp.

Why did the firefly keep crashing?

He wasn't very bright.

What game does a parrot like to play?

Hide and speak!

What do you get if you cross a tarantula with a rose?

I'm not sure, but don't try smelling it!

What do monkeys wear when they cook?

Ape-rons.

What's black and white and red all over?

A sunburned zebra!

What's brown and dangerous and lives in a tree?

A monkey with a carton of eggs!

What happened to the leopard that spent Christmas by the ocean?

It got sandy claws!

What do you call a lion that has eaten your dad's sister?

An aunt-eater!

Why don't bananas sunbathe?

Because they would peel.

What do you call a lion with no eyes?

Lon!

Is it hard to spot a leopard?

Not at all— they come that way!

What do toucans sing at Christmas?

Jungle Bells.

How did the monkey get down the stairs?

It slid down the banana-ster.

What do you call an explosive ape?

A baboom!

What does a toucan wear to go swimming?

A beak-ini!

How do you fix a broken chimp?

With a monkey wrench!

What goes grrr, squelch, grrr, squelch?

A lion in soggy shoes!

What do you get if you cross a snake with a builder?

A boa constructor!

What do you call a male zebra?

A ze-bro.

Why should you never tell a giraffe a secret?

Because you could fall off his neck as you whisper in his ear.

Why did the sick frog visit a hospital?

He needed a hop-eration!

Why shouldn't elephants visit the beach?

In case their trunks fall down!

What did the banana say to the gorilla?

Nothing, bananas can't talk!

Why couldn't the butterfly go to the dance?

Because it was a moth ball.

Did you hear about the rhino that caught a cold?

It became a rhi-snot-eros!

What did Tarzan tell his son?

"Be careful—it's a jungle out there."

Why was the baby ant confused?

Because all his uncles were ants!

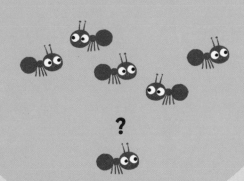

What is hairy and orange and always comes back to you?

A boomerang-utan.

Why couldn't the frog put down the book it was reading?

It was just too ribbit-ing!

Did you hear about the elephant that didn't matter?

It's irrelephant.

What does a kitten become after it's three days old?

Four days old.

What did one frog say to the other?

Time's sure fun when you're having flies!

Did you hear about the hippo at the North Pole?

It got hippothermia!

What sort of dancing will elephants do in your front room?

Break dancing!

What should a lizard do if it loses its tail?

Go to a retail outlet!

What's the most dangerous animal in your backyard?

The clothes-lion.

Did you hear about the snake's valentines card?

He sealed it with a hiss!

Did you hear about the cannibal lion?

He had to swallow his pride!

What game does a monkey like to play?

Hangman!

How do you start a firefly race?

On your marks, get set, glow!

What do you call an alligator detective?

An investi-gator.

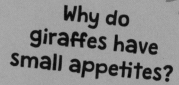

Why do giraffes have small appetites?

Because a little goes a long way.

Which animals were the last to leave Noah's Ark?

The elephants—they had to pack their trunks.

How do apes make cheese sandwiches?

They gorilla them!

What do you get if you cross a centipede and a parrot?

A walkie-talkie!

What's the most common music in the jungle?

Snake, rattle, and roll!

What do you get when you cross an elephant with a kangaroo?

Big holes all over Australia.

Why are tropical birds good at tennis?

Because toucan play at that game!

Where do you usually find sloths?

It depends where you left them!

Why do elephants never forget?

Because no one ever tells them anything.

Why does Tarzan shout so loudly?

Because it hurts when he pounds his chest.

What do you get if you cross a parrot and an elephant?

An animal that tells you everything it remembers!

Why do giraffes have such long necks?

Because their feet smell!

What toy did the baby snake have?

A rattle.

What has 99 legs and one eye?

A pirate centipede.

Why are elephants wrinkled?

Have you ever tried to iron one?

What has three trunks, two tails, and six feet?

An elephant with spare parts.

Why wouldn't the hyena play cards with the other animals?

Because one was a cheetah, and the other was lion!

What's the best time to buy parrots?

When they're going cheep.

How does the king of the jungle spend his days off?

Just lion around!

What did the lion cub say to its mother?

Every day I love you roar and roar!

Why did the leopard eat the tightrope walker?

He wanted a balanced diet.

Where did the leopard have its picnic?

It found just the right spot!

Baby Snake: Dad, are we poisonous?

Dad Snake: No, son, why do you ask?

Baby Snake: I've just bitten my tongue!

What is black and white and eats like a horse?

A zebra

Which of Jack Sparrow's feathered friends live in the jungle?

The Parrots of the Caribbean!

Which jungle creature tells the best jokes?

A stand-up chameleon.

What should you do if a rhino charges you?

Pay him!

FUN ON THE FARM

What do you call a factual TV show about sheep?

A flock-umentary!

What kind of animal goes "oom"?

A cow walking backward!

How did the pig with laryngitis feel?

Dis-gruntled.

What do you get if you cross a chicken with a kangaroo?

Pouched eggs!

What do you call a cow with only his two left legs?

Lean beef.

What has lots of ears, but can't hear anything at all?

A cornfield.

Why don't scarecrows eat?

They are already stuffed!

What has five fingers and drives a tractor?

A farm hand.

What did the waiter say when the horse walked into the café?

Why the long face?

Why do roosters curse all the time?

They are fowl-mouthed.

Why do cows moo?

Because their horns don't work!

Why did the goose cross the road?

To prove she wasn't chicken!

What do you get if you cross a donkey and Christmas?

Muletide greetings!

What do you call a sheep with no legs?

A cloud.

How did the farmer find his lost sheep?

He tractor down.

What do you call a boy who keeps rabbits?

Warren!

What did the duck say when she bought lipstick?

Put it on my bill!

What did the llama say when it was invited on holiday?

Alpaca my suitcase!

What did the polite sheep say to his friend at the gate?

After ewe.

What did the bee say when it returned to the hive?

"Honey, I'm home."

What do you give a sick pig?

Oinkment!

Where do cows go for history lessons?

To a mooseum!

What do you call a tale with a twist at the end?

A pigtail!

What do you call a sleeping bull?

A bulldozer.

If you had fifteen cows and five goats, what would you have?

Plenty of milk!

How many pigs do you need to make a smell?

A phew!

What do you get when you cross a rooster with a duck?

A bird that gets up at the quack of dawn.

What does it mean if you find a set of horse shoes?

Somewhere a horse is walking around in his socks!

What do you call a cow with an out-of-date map?

Udderly lost!

Why should you be careful where you step when it rains cats and dogs?

You could step in a poodle!

Doctor, I got trampled by a load of cows!

So I herd!

What's orange and sounds like a parrot?

A carrot.

What do horses tell their children at bedtime?

Pony tales!

How does a sheep finish a letter?

Sincerely ewes.

What's green and sings in the vegetable patch?

Elvis Parsley.

Why did the chicken cross the playground?

To get to the other slide!

When does a horse talk?

Whinny wants to!

What do you call a dog with a bunch of roses?

A collie-flower!

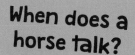

What do you get if you cross insects and a rabbit?

Bugs Bunny.

Why were the cows and sheep giggling?

Because they were laughing stock.

Why did the chicken run out onto the basketball court?

Because the referee whistled for a fowl!

Why did the farmer's dog keep chasing his tail?

He was trying to make ends meet.

Why do bees have icky, sticky hair?

They use honeycombs.

Why shouldn't you tell a secret on a farm?

Because the potatoes have eyes and the corn has ears!

Doctor, I feel like a goat!

Really? And how are the kids?

What do you call a pig with three eyes?

A piiig.

Why should you never tell your secrets to a piglet?

Because they might squeal!

How do you hire a farm worker?

Put a brick under each leg.

What did the pig say when the farmer grabbed him by the tail?

"That's the end of me."

Is chicken soup good for your health?

Not if you're the chicken!

Why did the boy stand behind the horse?

He thought he might get a kick out of it.

Why shouldn't you talk to rabbits about vegetables?

Because they don't carrot all!

What happened when the sheep pen broke?

The sheep had to use a pencil.

What grows down as it grows up?

A goose!

What do you get if you cross a cow and a jogging machine?

A milk shake!

What did the
chicken say when it
laid a square egg?

Owwww!

What sort of
jokes do chickens
like best?

Corny ones!

How do
hens dance?

Chick to chick!

What did the flamenco-dancing
farmer say to his chickens?

"Oh, lay!"

Why did the farmer set fire to the plants in his field?

He was growing baked beans!

What do you say to bees who try to steal honey?

Oh, beehive yourself!

Did you hear about the well-behaved cat?

It was purrfect.

What do you give a pony with a cold?

Cough stirrup!

Doctor, I feel like a dog!

How long have you felt that way?

Since I was a puppy!

Why did the farmer drive a steamroller over his field?

He wanted to grow mashed potatoes.

What do you get if you feed gunpowder to a chicken?

An egg-splosion!

Where do sheep get shorn?

At the baa-baas!

What says, "Moo, baa, woof, quack, meow, oink?"

A sheep that speaks foreign languages!

What do you get if you cross a cow with a camel?

Lumpy milkshakes!

Did you hear about the strawberry who attended charm school?

He became a real smoothie.

How can you tell if a cat likes the rain?

Because when it rains, it purrs!

SILLY SEALIFE

What did the fisherman say to the magician?

"Pick a cod, any cod."

What kind of fish likes to eat between meals?

A snackerel.

Which country has the most dolphins?

Finland.

How did the octopus make the dolphin laugh?

With ten tickles!

What's the best way
to stuff a lobster?

Take it out for pizza
and ice cream.

Which fish are the best at
home-improvement projects?

Hammerhead sharks.

Which sea creatures
are the biggest
cry babies?

Whales.

What fish do knights like best?

Swordfish.

What musical instrument are fish afraid of?

Casta-nets!

Why wouldn't the crab twins share their rock pool?

Because they're two shellfish!

What do you call a lazy shrimp?

A slobster!

Why do fish in a school all swim in the same direction?

They're playing Salmon Says!

What do you call a baby squid?

A little squirt.

Where does a squid keep its money?

In an octopurse.

Why did the lobster blush?

Because the sea weed!

What can fly underwater?

A mosquito in a submarine.

43

Why wasn't the octopus afraid of being attacked?

It was well-armed!

How does a penguin feel when it is left all alone?

Ice-olated.

What did Cinderella wear when she went diving?

Glass flippers.

How do fish get to school?

By octobus.

44

What do
whales like
to chew?

Blubber gum.

What lies at
the bottom of
the ocean and
won't move?

A nervous wreck!

Why don't oysters
like loud music?

Because a noisy
noise annoys
an oyster!

What did the diver
shout when he swam into
a seaweed forest?

"Kelp!"

What's that gooey stuff in between a shark's teeth?

Slow swimmers!

How do you get in touch with a fish?

You drop it a line!

What do you get if you meet a shark in the Arctic Ocean?

Frostbite.

Why did the burglar buy a surfboard?

He wanted to start a crime wave!

Which salad ingredient is the most dangerous for ocean liners?

Iceberg lettuce.

What do you call a man floating up and down on the sea?

Bob.

Which bird is always out of breath?

A puffin!

What kind of jokes do sea turtles tell?

Shell-arious ones!

Which sea creature wants to be left alone?

A hermit crab!

What do the underwater police travel in?

Squid cars!

Why are fish easy to weigh?

Because they have their own scales.

Which sea creature eats its prey
two at a time?

Noah's shark!

What day do fish hate?

Fry day.

Why do
whales sing?

Because they
can't talk!

What did
the walrus do
after he read
the sad book?

He started
to blubber.

How did the dolphin
get to the hospital?

In a clambulance.

What's the biggest danger for fishermen?

Pulling a mussel!

Which fish come out at night?

Starfish.

Why did the young stingray want to chat with his dad?

He wanted to have a manta-man talk.

What are baby sea creatures most afraid of?

Squid-nappers!

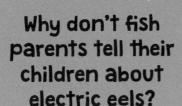

Why don't fish parents tell their children about electric eels?

They're just too shocking.

Which game is popular with fish?

Name That Tuna.

What is the saddest creature in the ocean?

The blue whale!

What did the fish say when he swam into the concrete wall?

Dam!

What do sea captains tell their children at night?

Ferry tales.

What game do jellyfish play at parties?

Tide and seek!

What do you get when you cross a shark and a snowman?

Frostbite!

What can you expect from a clever crab?

Snappy answers!

Why do seahorses live in salt water?

Because pepper water makes them sneeze!

What do you call a baby crab?

A little nipper!

Why was no one able to play cards on Noah's Ark?

Because Noah stood on the deck!

What did the crab say to her grouchy husband?

"Don't get snappy with me!"

What does a turtle do on its birthday?

It shellebrates!

What kind of fish are useful in cold weather?

Skates.

Why do penguins carry fish in their beaks?

Because they don't have any pockets!

What vegetables do sailors hate?

Leeks!

Where can you find an ocean with no water?

On a map.

What do you call two matching penguins?

Pengtwins!

What happened when the boat carrying red paint crashed into one carrying blue paint?

Both crews were marooned.

Why did the shark
bang its head against the
bottom of the ship?

It was a hammerhead!

Where do you
find starfish?

In the
Galack Sea!

Why did the man
go swimming in
his best clothes?

He thought he
needed a wet suit.

How do dolphins decide who
goes first?

They flipper coin!

What is in the middle of a jellyfish?

Its jellybutton!

What happened when the tuna went to Hollywood?

He became a starfish.

How can you tell that the ocean is feeling friendly?

It keeps waving at you.

Where do fish sleep?

On a waterbed!

What does an octopus wear in winter?

A coat of arms!

Why did the jellyfish cross the ocean?

To get to the other tide!

Why are fish so clever?

They swim in schools!

Which two fish can you wear on your feet?

A sole and an eel.

What music do they play in underwater nightclubs?

Sole music!

Why don't fish play tennis?

Because they are afraid of the net.

What did the beach say to the wave?

Long tide, no sea!

How do you close an envelope underwater?

With a seal.

CLASSROOM CAPERS

Why did the firefly get bad test results?

It wasn't very bright!

What is a butterfly's best subject?

Moth-ematics!

Dad: What did you learn in school today, Bella?

Bella: Not enough, I have to go back tomorrow!

Why did the teacher visit the optician?

She couldn't control her pupils!

Teacher: When things go wrong, what can you always count on?

Sally: Your fingers?

Why did the boy eat his homework?

His teacher said it was a piece of cake!

Which snakes are good at maths?

Adders!

Teacher: Luke, why haven't you done your homework?

Luke: Sorry, I'm reading a book on glue, and I just couldn't put it down!

Why did the music teacher bring a ladder to class?

So her students could reach the high notes!

What kind of bus takes you through school, not to school?

A sylla-bus!

Why couldn't the geometry teacher go to school?

She'd sprained her angle!

What breed of dog does a science teacher like best?

A lab!

Teacher: Who invented fractions?

Pupil: Henry the Eighth!

What subject do athletes like the best?

Jog-raphy!

Why couldn't the student write an essay on fish?

He didn't have any waterproof ink!

Teacher: Have you been stupid all your life?

Andrew: Not yet!

What's worse than finding a worm in your fruit?

Finding half a worm!

Why was the clock in the school cafeteria slow?

Because it always went back four seconds.

What do history teachers talk about at parties?

The good old days!

Why did the school janitor hate the basketball team?

Because of all the dribbling on court!

Dad: And how did the exams go today?

Kevin: I got 100%.

Dad: That's great. Which subjects?

Kevin: 50% in history and 50% in geography.

What do a burger and a high school teacher have in common?

They're both pro-teen!

Teacher: What's a computer byte?

Samantha: I don't know. I didn't even know that a computer had teeth!

Teacher: Emily, why does your homework look like your dad wrote it?

Emily: Because I used his pen?

What happens if you throw a pile of books into the ocean?

You get a title wave!

What did the pencil say to the protractor?

Take me to your ruler.

Why aren't there desks in the mathematics classroom?

Because they use times tables!

What tool does an arithmetic teacher use the most?

Multi-pliers!

Pupil: Sorry I'm late. I overslept.

Teacher: What, you mean you sleep at home as well?

Teacher: Do you know why your grades are so bad?

Nathan: I can't think.

Teacher: Exactly!

Teacher: Where would you find a cowboy?

Max: In a field—and stop calling me "boy"!

Why did the science teacher remove his doorbell?

He wanted to win the no-bell prize!

Why did the boy bring a surfboard to school?

The teacher said they were going to be surfing the internet.

What kind of dinosaur knows the most words?

A thesaurus!

Why do classrooms have bright lights?

Because the students are so dim!

Teacher: Simon, can you say your name backward?

Simon: No, miss!

Why was the technology teacher late for school?

He had a hard drive!

Teacher: What's the definition of asymmetry?

Student: A place where you bury dead people.

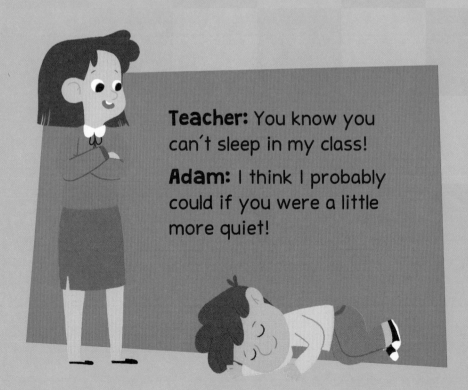

Teacher: You know you can't sleep in my class!

Adam: I think I probably could if you were a little more quiet!

What did the science teacher say before he got into a fight?

Let me atom!

How do you make 1 into 0?

Add a "g" at the beginning, and it's gone!

Why was everyone locked out of the music room?

Because the keys were on the piano!

Teacher: Did you know that most accidents happen in the kitchen?

Pupil: Yes, but we still have to eat them!

Where does the school furniture go to dance?

The local desk-o!

Why was 6 afraid of 7?

Because 7 8 9!

Teacher: Jake, your essay on "My dog" is exactly the same as your sister's.

Jake: I know, Miss. It's the same dog.

What's the tastiest class at school?

History. It's full of dates.

Which animal can't be trusted during exams?

The cheetah!

Why are baby goats so good at long division?

They're smart kids!

Teacher: Did your mother help you with your homework?

Charlie: No, I got it wrong all by myself!

Did you hear about the unhappy algebra book?

It had too many problems.

What did the music teacher say to the two students who wouldn't perform together?

Just duet!

Which vegetables do school librarians like best?

Quiet peas!

Teacher: Sammy, you missed school yesterday, didn't you?

Sammy: Not really!

How do you impress an art teacher?

Easel-y!

Why did the mathematics teacher have an old-fashioned alarm clock?

She liked arithma-ticks!

Why did the teacher write on the window?

She wanted her lesson to be clear.

Teacher: Mitchell, I hope I didn't see you looking at Tyler's exam paper?
Mitchell: I hope you didn't, too!

What do a cookie and a computer have in common?

They both have chips!

How do you get straight As?

By using a ruler!

Dad: Did you come first in any of your school subjects?

Daisy: No, but I was first out of the classroom when the bell rang!

Why didn't the nose want to go to school?

It got picked on!

What did the pencil sharpener say to the pencil?

Stop going around in circles, and get to the point!

Why did the art teacher get suspended?

She didn't know where to draw the line!

Why did the school cafeteria hire a dentist?

To make more filling meals!

Lily: Our teacher talks to herself.

Milly: So does ours, but she thinks we're listening!

What did the vegetarian teacher say at lunchtime?

Lettuce eat our salads now!

Dad: Lucy, why are your history grades so low?

Lucy: They keep asking about things that happened before I was born!

Teacher: Mike, your ideas are like diamonds.

Mike: What, they are beautiful and precious?

Teacher: No, they're extremely rare!

Miss Addison: Michelle, are those new glasses?

Michelle: Yes, I'm hoping they'll improve di-vision!

Why is the library a school's tallest building?

Because it has the most stories!

Teacher: What is the shortest month?

Khalid: May. It only has three letters!

How do you know your school bus is old?

When the seats are covered in mammoth hide!

Teacher: Sleep is really good for the brain.

Martina: Then why can't we sleep in class?

Teacher: Anyone who hasn't done their homework will be in big trouble.

Joe: How can we get in trouble for something we didn't do?

What did the number 0 say to the number 8?

"That's a cool belt."

What's worse than taking an exam?

Finding out the grade.

Did you hear about the girl who took the school bus home?

Her parents made her take it back!

Chloe: I wish I'd been born a thousand years ago.

Teacher: Why's that?

Chloe: There would be a lot less history to learn!

Why did the student go to the arithmetic class?

To make up the numbers!

What kind of cake do you get in the school cafeteria?

A stomach-cake!

When are you allowed to take bubblegum to school?

On chews-day!

Why did the student walk to school facing the wrong way?

It was "back-to-school day"!

SCHOOL

Teacher: I'd like to go through a whole lesson without telling you off.

Sam: Be my guest!

How is an English teacher like a judge?

They both give out sentences!

Teacher: Imani, which hand do you write with?

Imani: I don't write with my hand. I write with a pen!

HILARIOUS HOBBIES

What kind of parties do snowboarders go to?

Snowballs.

What sport does King Kong like to play?

Ping Pong!

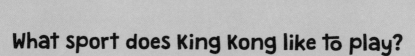

Did you hear about the nun who wanted to play football?

She was trying to kick the habit!

What kinds of stories do basketball players tell?

Tall tales!

What do you call a very clever tennis player?

A racket scientist!

What do skiers eat for breakfast?

Frosted Flakes!

What do skiers eat for lunch?

Icebergers!

Why was Cinderella terrible at basketball?

Because her coach was a pumpkin!

What should you do when the basketball court is flooded?

Bring on the subs!

You can't fish here, this is a private lake!

I'm not fishing, I'm teaching my pet worm to swim!

Why shouldn't you cycle on an empty stomach?

Because it's easier on a bicycle.

What animal is always at a baseball game?

A bat!

Why is a doughnut like a golfer?

It has a hole in one!

What sport do horses like best?

Stable tennis!

What's the quietest sport?

Bowling, because you can hear a pin drop!

What did the martial artist buy from the butcher?

Karate chops!

Why don't tuna play tennis?

They don't want to get caught in the net!

What do you do when you see an elephant with a basketball?

Get out of the way!

What game do snowboarders like to play?

Ice Spy with my little eye ...

Why do astronauts make good football players?

They know how to make a great touchdown!

What drink do soccer players like least?

Penal-tea!

Why didn't the dog want to play football?

It was a boxer!

What's better than juggling swords?

Having fingers!

Why did the racing car driver make so many pit stops?

He kept asking for directions!

What race is never run?

A swimming race!

What goes in pink and comes out blue?

A pig going for a swim in winter!

Which part of a swimming pool is never the same?

The changing rooms!

Did you hear about the magician that lost his temper on stage?

He pulled his hare out!

Why would you take a baseball glove on a surfing trip?

So you can catch a wave!

Why can't waiters play tennis?

They only want to serve!

What part of a soccer stadium smells the nicest?

The scenter spot!

Which ballet do pigs like best?

Swine Lake.

Why didn't the almonds go to the ballet?

Because they were afraid of The Nutcracker!

Why can't elephants dance?

They have two left feet!

How is a baseball team similar to a pancake?

They both need a good batter!

What did the baseball glove say to the baseball?

Catch you later!

Why are meteors very good at soccer?

Because they're shooting stars!

Why shouldn't you build a fire in a kayak?

You can't have your kayak and heat it!

What game do tornadoes like to play?

Twister!

What can you serve, but not eat?

A tennis ball!

Why did the boy keep doing the backstroke?

Because he'd just eaten and he didn't want to swim on a full stomach!

Why didn't the ice skater get married?

He got cold feet!

What did the jockey say when she fell off her horse?

"I can't giddy-up!"

What do you call a superhero playing baseball?

Batman!

What runs around a baseball field but never moves?

The fence!

What game does an astronaut like to play?

Moon-opoly!

Did you hear about the magician that threw his watch up in the air?

He wanted to see time fly!

How can you tell that a cheerleader is nervous?

She's jumpy.

What food does an athlete like best?

Runner beans!

Why did the basketball player always have cookies with his drink?

So he could dunk them!

What letter of the alphabet does a golfer like best?

Tee!

What did the golfer eat for lunch?

A sand wedge.

Which volleyball player wears the biggest shoes?

The one with the biggest feet!

What kind of cats go bowling?

Alley cats!

What do you call a nervous javelin thrower?

Shakespeare!

Which figure skater can jump higher than the judges' table?

All of them—a table can't jump.

Why did the basketball player go to the doctor?

To get his shots!

Why did the soccer player oversleep?

He was dreaming about playing a game and it went into extra time!

Which hobby do dogs like?

Collecting fleas.

Why is a sports stadium always cold?

Because it's full of fans!

When is a basketball player like a baby?

When he dribbles!

Why did the boy win the big the race?

He had athlete's foot!

What do snowboarders do
when they meet someone new?

They try to break the ice.

What sport do
insects play?

Cricket!

Why was the
swimmer
so slow?

He could only
do the crawl!

What is harder
to catch
the further
you run?

Your breath!

Why do penguins make good racing car drivers?

Because they're always in pole position!

Why did Tarzan spend so much time on the golf course?

He was perfecting his swing.

Where do old bowling balls end up?

The gutter!

Why did the jogger eat on the run?

She loved fast food!

Why is a slow racing driver like a bowl of milk?

He keeps getting lapped!

Did you hear about the artist who was pinned to the ground by wooden frames?

He'd come down with easels!

Why did the hockey puck quit?

It was tired of being pushed around!

What do you call a cat that plays football?

Puss in boots!

Why can't you play soccer with pigs?

Because they always hog the ball!

When is the best time to enter the high jump?

When it's a leap year!

If an athlete suffers from athlete's foot, what does an astronaut suffer from?

Missile-toe!

Why was the basketball player dropped from the team?

She had lost her bounce!

Why did the ninja spend a week in bed?

He had kung flu!

Did you hear about the magician that disappeared during his act?

He was going through a stage!

What do you get if you cross a bad golfer and a broken-down car?

Something that goes, "Putt, putt, putt, putt."

Why did the gardener plant a light bulb?

She wanted to grow a power plant!

Why didn't the tennis player change the light bulb?

He refused to admit it was out!

Why was the soccer game played on a triangle?

Somebody took a corner!

Why did the tired athlete run around and around her bed?

To catch up on some sleep!

TRAVEL TEASERS

What do you call a family that takes their own salt and pepper everywhere they travel?

Seasoned tourists!

What's the best thing to do on a trip to the Arctic?

Just chill.

What do you call a train with a cold?

Achoo-choo train!

What did the sailor think as he fell overboard?

Water way to go!

Why did the train driver get fired?

He was too easily side-tracked!

What's the best medicine for seasickness?

Vitamin sea!

Why couldn't the astronaut land on the Moon?

Because it was full!

Why do seagulls live by the sea?

Because if they lived by the bay, they'd be bagels!

What do you need to drive your car along the beach?

Four-eel drive!

Where do penguins go to vote?

The South Poll!

How do you get a baby astronaut to sleep?

Rocket!

Why did the cyclist get a puncture?

He didn't see the fork in the road!

What's fluffy and green?

A seasick poodle.

When is a sailor like a plank of wood?

When he's aboard!

Why is it hard to learn your alphabet on a cruise?

Because you spend so much time at C!

Why should you avoid fruitcake when you're on a boat?

It may contain dangerous currants!

Why was the thirsty astronaut hanging out near the computer keyboard?

He was looking for the space bar.

What do you call a happy one-legged pirate?

A hop-timist!

Which country is full of people crying and sobbing?

Wales!

What do astronauts eat out of?

Satellite dishes.

Why do chefs go to Italy for their holidays?

To see the Leaning Tower of Pizza!

Where is Hadrian's Wall?

Around Hadrian's garden!

Did you hear about the cuddly sea captain?

He liked to hug the shore!

How do you know if a train has gone past?

Look for the tracks!

Why don't elephants travel by train?

They don't like putting their trunks on the luggage rack!

What's fluffy and green?

A seasick sheep!

Where do pianists go for some sunshine?

The Florida Keys!

What kind of pizza do dogs order?

Pupperoni!

How does a penguin travel across the ice?

It just goes with the floe!

What is the capital of Australia?

A!

Where do eggs go for a weekend break?

New Yolk!

What sort of food can you buy on a Chinese boat?

Junk food!

What did the Pacific ocean say to the Atlantic ocean?

Nothing, it just waved!

Where can you find the Andes?

At the end of your armies!

What happened when the monkey ate the safari guide's joke book?

He felt funny.

What do you get if you run behind a car?

Exhausted!

On which day do lions eat the most safari tourists?

Chewsday

What did one mountain say to the other?

"You're looking a little peaky!"

What do they sing on your birthday in Iceland?

"Freeze a jolly good fellow!"

Which state sneezes the most?

Mass-achoo-setts!

What's brown, hairy, and wears sunglasses?

A coconut at the beach!

What's the best way to cross the ocean?

By taxi-crab!

What did the cruise liner say as it sailed into port?

"What's up, dock?"

Which beach item gets wetter the more it dries?

A towel.

Winnie: Why is there a plane outside your bedroom door?

Vinnie: I must have left the landing light on!

What happened to the man who took the 5 o'clock train home?

He had to give it back!

What does an astronaut have in the back of the car?

A booster seat!

Can you name five animals found at the South Pole?

Four penguins and a seal!

When is a boat like a pile of snow?

When it's adrift!

What do you use to cut the ocean in two?

A seasaw!

What falls at the North Pole but never gets hurt?

Snow!

What happens when you throw a white rock into the Red Sea?

It gets wet!

What has four wheels and flies?

A garbage truck!

What is the fastest country in the world?

Rusha!

What keeps on running without getting tired?

A river!

Why do astronauts take sandwiches
on board their rocket?

They get hungry at launch time!

What do you
say to a frog that's
hitching a ride?

"Hop in!"

What has big
ears, four legs,
and a trunk?

A mouse with its
luggage.

What did one
beach say to the
other beach?

"Show me your
mussels!"

Which animal was the first in space?

The cow who jumped over the moon!

What do you get if you meet a shark in the Arctic Ocean?

Frostbite!

What item is still in fashion for train passengers?

Platform shoes!

What do you call a Frenchman wearing sandals?

Philippe Flop!

What's the best car for driving through water?

A Ford!

How do elephants travel long distances?

In jumbo jets!

What sort of boats do clever students travel on?

Scholar-ships!

What's the best day for sailing?

Winds-day!

Why should you never argue on a hot-air balloon ride?

You don't want to
fall out!

How do you get ice off a hot-air balloon?

You use a
skyscraper!

Where do cows spend the night when they're away from home?

A moo-tel!

How do lighthouse keepers communicate with each other?

With shine language!

FUNNY FOLK

What do clowns wear to go swimming?

Giggles!

Why did the gardener quit her job?

Because her celery wasn't high enough!

Doctor, I dreamed last night that I'd turned into a deck of cards.

I'll deal with you later!

Why did grandpa put wheels on his rocking chair?

He wanted to rock and roll!

What do you say to someone sitting on your roof?

"High!"

What happened to the man who plugged his electric blanket into the toaster?

He kept popping out of bed all night!

My sister is so dumb, she went to the dentist to get her Bluetooth fixed!

What do you call a man with pockets full of dry leaves?

Russell!

Waiter, there's a twig in my meal!

Just a moment, sir, I'll get the branch manager.

Doctor, I keep running around pretending to be a seabird.

No wonder you're puffin!

Dad: You shouldn't play ball today, son. You have a sickness bug.

Leo: I know, I keep throwing up!

Charlie: Why does your mother wear two sweaters for golf?

Carly: In case she gets a hole in one!

Kurt: What has four legs, spots, and smells bad?

Bert: Me and my brother!

Dad, I keep thinking I'm a woodworm!

Well, life does get boring sometimes!

Annie: Your aunt looks so old!

Danny: Yes, she's an aunt-ique!

Bill: How do you keep your pet rabbits looking so good?

Will: I use a hare brush!

Nick: My dad had to go to court for stealing a calendar.

Rick: What happened?

Nick: He got twelve months!

Doctor, I swallowed a bone.

Are you choking?

No, I really did!

Karen: I wish you would only sing Christmas carols.

Aaron: Aw, thanks. Do you like me singing them most of all?

Karen: No, but I would only have to hear you sing once a year!

Christine: My dad can juggle eggshells, yesterday's newspaper, and an empty box!

Eugene: That's garbage!

Dad: You've been walking sideways ever since you came home from the hospital.

Hannah: They said my medicine might have side effects!

Did you hear about the explosion at the French cheese factory?

Yes, all that was left was de Brie!

Ned: Why is the light always on in your brother's room?

Fred: Because he's so dim!

Flo: Why are you crying and chewing at the same time?

Joe: I just swallowed some blubber gum!

What do you call a man with his head in a saucepan?

Stu!

Why did the clown call the doctor?

Because he broke his funny bone!

Doctor, I think I'm a dog!

How long have you felt like this?

Ever since I was a puppy!

Why did the baker get fired from her job?

She was a loafer!

Chris: My dad's an undertaker.

Fliss: Does he enjoy it?

Chris: Of corpse he does!

My brother is so stupid, he drinks hot chocolate at night so he will have sweet dreams!

Dad: There's a burglar downstairs eating the cake your sister baked.

Sam: Should I call the police or an ambulance?

Little Sister: Why is our goldfish orange?

Big brother: Because the water makes it rusty!

Doctor, I keep hearing a ringing sound!

Then answer your phone, silly!

Danny: Ma, she's stolen the yolk from my egg!

Annie: Shh, it's all white now!

What's the best time to go to the dentist?

Tooth-hurty (2:30)!

Dad: Eliza, did you put the cat out?

Eliza: I didn't need to. It wasn't on fire!

What's the difference between a well-dressed gentleman and an exhausted dog?

One wears an expensive suit and the other just pants.

Why are grandpa's teeth like stars?

Because they come out at night!

What do you call someone who loves hot chocolate?

A cocoa-nut!

Where do ice cream sellers learn their trade?

At sundae school.

What is an archeologist?

Someone whose career is in ruins.

Doctor, no matter what I do, I just can't get to sleep!

Lie on the edge of the bed, and you'll soon drop off.

Grandma: What do you want to be when you grow up, dear?

Lewis: I'm aspirin' to be a pharmacist!

Dad: What happened to your amazing five-day diet?

Edward: I finished all the food in two days!

What's the difference between a boring parent and a boring book?

You can shut the book up!

Gran: Why are you eating that BLT in the bathtub?

Ewan: It's a sub sandwich!

What did the ninja say to the doctor?

Hi-ya!

Which food do mathematicians like best?

Square-root vegetables!

Did you hear about the girl who was smacked in the face by a frisbee?

She wondered why it was getting bigger ... and then it hit her!

What do you call a man with a car on his head?

Jack!

Arthur: I don't like cheese with holes!

Dad: Well, eat the cheese and leave the holes on the side of your plate.

Matt: Why did your mother quit her job at the can crushing plant?

Kat: Because it was soda pressing!

Dad: Why do your shoes look like bananas?

Harriet: They're my slippers!

Katy: Dad, how can I join the police?

Dad: Handcuff them all together!

Did you hear about the man who swallowed his money?

The doctor was looking for signs of change.

Doctor, I think I need glasses.

I agree, this is a fast-food restaurant.

Grandma: Eat your greens, Malik. They're good for your skin.

Malik: But I don't want green skin!

When are your eyes not your eyes?

When a cold wind makes them water!

Kim: Why is your drawing of a fish so tiny?

Tim: I've drawn it to scale!

What do you call a man that blocks a river?

Adam!

My aunt has one leg longer than the other.

Is she called Eileen?

137

What did the weather woman use to curl her hair?

A heat wave!

Stacey: I was given an x-ray by my dentist yesterday.

Casey: A tooth pic?

Alan: Is my supper ready? I have karate class in an hour.

Dad: Your chops are on the table!

Why do kids listen to music on long trips?

Because car-toons keep them happy!

Why can't you hear a psychiatrist go to the bathroom?

Because the P is silent!

When does a doctor get angry?

When she runs out of patients!

Why was the chef so relaxed?

She had plenty of thyme on her hands!

Why did the girl stare at the carton of orange juice?

It said "concentrate" on the label.

Where do people get their medicine in the countryside?

From a farmer-cist!

What did the burglar's daughter play with at bathtime?

A robber ducky!

Hey, what's this spider doing on my ice cream?

Skiing?

Did you hear that Uncle Bob lost his wig on the roller coaster?

It was a hair-raising ride!

Why did the inventor stuff herbs in the disk drive of his computer?

He was trying to build a thyme machine.

Benny: My stupid brother tried to catch fog yesterday.

Lenny: I bet he mist...

Mickey: Our mother has named us all after members of our family.

Nicky: Is that why your big brother is called Uncle Joe?

What sort of dog is good at looking after children?

A baby setter.

Carrie: How did your Dad get injured on his fishing trip?

Harry: He pulled a mussel!

What do you call a woman with one leg on either side of a river?

Bridget!

How do you make antifreeze?

Hide her coat and gloves!

Why does your sister put glue on her salad?

She wants to stick to her diet!

How did the musical farmer know which note to sing?

He used a pitchfork!

Dad, I can't mow the lawn today, I've twisted my ankle.

That's a lame excuse!

Doctor, I keep thinking I'm a spider.

Sounds like a web of lies to me.

Why didn't the boy tell the doctor he'd swallowed some glue?

His lips were sealed!

Did you hear about the thief who went to the doctor because she couldn't sleep?

The doctor gave her a mat and told her to lie low for a while.

What do you call a boy with a seagull on his head?

Cliff!

Doctor, I feel like a sharp pencil.

I see your point!

Why shouldn't you argue with a weatherman?

He might storm out on you!

Molly: Have you put some more water in the goldfish bowl?

Holly: No. It still hasn't drunk the water I put in when I first bought it!

Dad: Why did you kick your brother in the stomach?

Sally: It was an accident. I meant to kick his back, but he turned around!

What did the boy say after reading for too long in the sun?

"I'm certainly well red!"

My cousin is so stupid, he took his computer to the nurse because it had a virus!

OUT OF THIS WORLD

Did you hear about the robot dog?

His megabark was worse than his megabyte.

How do you get rid of stinky ghosts?

With scare freshener!

What do you get if you cross a skeleton and a dog?

An animal that buries itself!

What did the vampire say to the invisible man?

Long time, no see!

What kind of music do mummies like?

Wrap music!

Why did the dragon join a gym?

It wanted to burn some calories!

How high do witches fly?

Way up in the atmos-fear!

Why are aliens green?

Because they're not ripe yet!

What do Italian ghosts eat for dinner?

Spookhetti!

What kind of monsters love to dance to pop music?

The boogie-men!

What goes "ha ha, thunk?"

A monster laughing its head off!

What type of witch can help you see in the dark?

A lights-witch.

Where did the zombie go to swim?

The Dead Sea!

Why is it difficult to tell twin witches apart?

Because you don't know which witch is which!

How do vampires wash themselves?

They get in the bat tub!

What do you get if you cross a wizard with a spaceship?

A flying sorcerer!

Did you hear about the witch in the five-star hotel?

She ordered broom service!

What board game do zombies avoid?

The Game of Life!

Who saves drowning spirits at the seaside?

The ghostguard!

What did the ghost write in his girlfriend's valentine card?

You're simply boo-tiful!

Where do mermaids go to see movies?

The dive-in.

Why don't giants speak to leprechauns?

They're no good at small talk.

What does a troll drive?

A monster truck!

What advice should you always give to robots?

Look before you bleep!

What do you say to a French skeleton?

Bone-jour!

What time of day do zombies like best?

Ate o'clock!

Did you hear about the witch who turned green?

She got broom sick on long journeys!

What's the best place to talk to a monster?

From as far away as possible!

What did the little ghost say to his best friend?

"Do you believe in people?"

Which fruit do vampires like to eat?

Neck-tarines!

What are vampires most afraid of?

Tooth decay!

Why should you never lie to a monster with x-ray vision?

Because it can see right through you!

Why did the mermaid ride a sea horse?

Because she was playing water polo!

What do you call a wizard who's really good at golf?

Harry Putter.

What did the werewolf say to the skeleton?

It's been nice gnawing you!

What do you call a fairy that has never taken a bath?

Stinkerbell!

How can you tell when there's a giant monster under your bed?

When your nose touches the ceiling.

How do you reach the second floor of a haunted house?

Climb up the monstairs!

How do monster stories begin?

"Once upon a slime ..."

How can you tell if a skeleton owns an umbrella?

It's bone dry!

What did the vampire say to his dentist?

Fangs very much!

How do you stop a robot from biting its nails?

Replace them with screws!

Do monsters eat snacks with their fingers?

No, they eat the fingers separately.

Who's the most important player on a monster soccer team?

The ghoul keeper!

What do you call an alien with five eyes?

An Aliiiiien!

What kind of hair do mermaids have?

Wavy!

On what day was the hairy monster born?

Fursday!

Why did Dracula take cold medicine?

To keep from coffin!

Why were the vampires upside down?

They were just hanging out!

What do ghosts wash their hair with?

Sham-boo!

Where's the safest place to hide from a zombie?

In the living room!

What does a mermaid use her phone for?

To take shelfies!

How do you get a robot to come to a party?

Send it a tin-vitation!

Why do skeletons find it easy to stay calm?

Because nothing gets under their skin!

What does Dracula do in the summer?

He goes vamping!

What do zombies play in the playground?

Corpses and robbers!

Why didn't the skeleton go to the party?

It had no body to go with!

What do little vampires eat?

Alpha-bat soup!

Why did the cyclops' school close down?

Because it only had one pupil!

Why did the witch buy a computer?

She needed a spell-checker!

What do you call a sprite with a twisted ankle?

A hobblin' goblin!

Why was Dracula thrown out of his art class?

He could only draw blood.

Did you hear about the poltergeist in the china shop?

It had a smashing time!

What happened to the witch who swallowed a poisonous toad?

She croaked!

161

Why does Peter Pan fly everywhere?

He Neverlands!

Which sweet treats do aliens like best?

Martian-mallows!

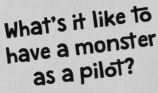

What's it like to have a monster as a pilot?

Terror-flying!

How do you know the skull won the race?

It was definitely ahead!

What do monsters eat at a party?

Eyes-cream!

What's the best way to greet a werewolf?

"Howl do you do?"

What's as sharp and pointed as one of Dracula's fangs?

The other one!

Why did the fairy move out of the toadstool?

Because there wasn't mushroom.

BACK IN TIME

What is the first thing a queen does when she ascends the throne?

She sits down.

Where did Napoleon keep his armies?

Up his sleevies

What do you call a prehistoric monster when it is asleep?

A dino-snore.

Did Adam and Eve ever have a date?

No, but they had an apple!

What did Robin Hood wear to the Sherwood Forest ball?

A bow tie.

What was written on the knight's tomb?

"May he rust in peace."

When did early people start wearing uncreased clothes?

In the Iron Age!

Where does a Tyrannosaurus sit when he comes to stay?

Anywhere he wants to.

Who made dinner for Robin Hood and his Merry Men?

Frier Tuck

Why did Columbus cross the ocean?

To get to the other tide.

Which knight designed King Arthur's Round Table!

Sir Cumference!

Where did the pirate keep his boat?

In the harrrbor.

What happened to the knight who lost his left arm and left leg in battle?

He was all right in the end.

What do Alexander the Great and Billy the Kid have in common?

The same middle name.

How did Vikings send secret messages?

By Norse code.

What did King Henry VIII do whenever he burped?

He issued a royal pardon.

Which dinosaur can't stay out of the rain?

A Stegosaur-rust!

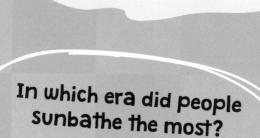

In which era did people sunbathe the most?

The Bronzed Age.

Where do Egyptian mummies go for a swim?

To the Dead Sea.

Why did Eve move to New York?

She fell for the Big Apple.

Why did the very first fries not taste very nice?

Because they were fried in ancient Greece!

Where did Viking teachers send sick children?

To the school Norse.

Why do historians believe that Rome was built at night?

Because it wasn't built in a day.

What snack did the caveman like best?

A club sandwich.

What do you call a blind dinosaur?

Doyouthinkhesaurus.

What did Mount Vesuvius say to Pompeii?

I lava you.

Did prehistoric people hunt bear?

No, they wore clothes!

Why did the mammoth have a woolly coat?

Because it would have looked silly in a parka.

How did the pirate get his Jolly Roger so cheaply?

He bought it on sail.

What did Columbus do after he crossed the Atlantic?

He dried his clothes.

Which king had the largest crown?

The one with the biggest head!

Why did Cleopatra take milk baths?

She couldn't find a cow tall enough for her to take a shower.

Two wrongs don't make a right, but what do two rights make?

The first aircraft!

What did the caveman give his girlfriend on Valentine's Day?

Ugs and kisses.

What music do Egyptian mummies like best?

Wrap music!

Who was the fastest runner of all time?

Adam, because he was first in the human race!

Why was England so wet in the nineteenth century?

Because Queen Victoria's reign lasted 64 years.

Why did King Arthur have a Round Table?

So that no one could corner him.

Why was the pharoah so boastful?

He sphinx he's the best.

What did Robin Hood say when he was almost hit at the archery tournament?

"That was an arrow escape!"

Why did Captain Cook sail to Australia?

It was too far to swim.

What should you do if you see a caveman?

Go inside and explore, man!

Why did the mammoth have a trunk?

Because it would have looked silly with suitcases.

First Roman Soldier: What's the time?

Second Roman Soldier: XV past VIII.

First Roman Soldier: By the time I work that out, it will be midnight!

What did the ancient Egyptians call bad leaders?

Un-Pharaohs.

What was Noah's job?

He was an ark-itect.

What did the executioner say to the former king?

It's time to head off!

What sort of music did cavemen enjoy?

Rock music!

What's purple and 5,000 miles long?

The grape wall of China.

What does the Statue of Liberty stand for?

It can't sit down.

What do dinosaurs have that no other creatures have?

Baby dinosaurs.

What happened when electricity was discovered?

Someone got a nasty shock.

What happened when the wheel was invented?

It caused a revolution.